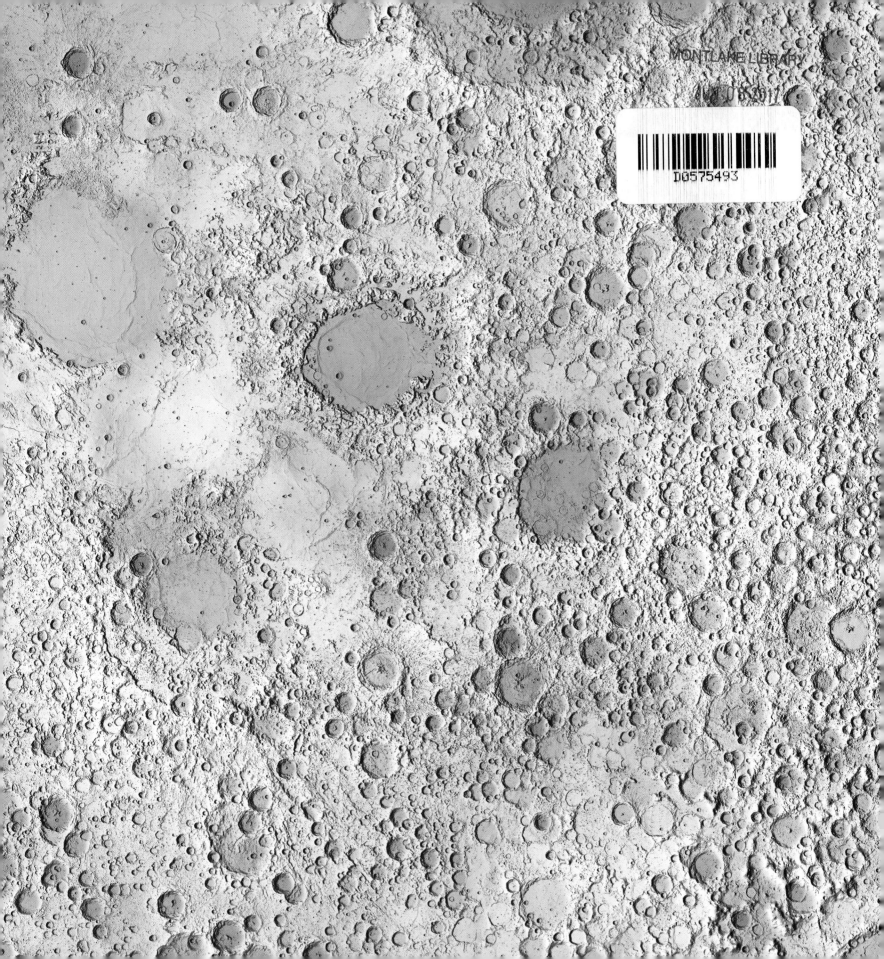

moonwalk

First published in 2016 by Circa Press
©2016 Circa Press Limited

Circa Press
50 Great Portland Street
London W1W 7ND
www.circapress.net

ISBN 978-0-9930721-7-8

Printed and bound in Latvia

Reproduction: DawkinsColour
Design: Jean-Michel Dentand

moonwalk

The Story of the Apollo 11 Moon Landing

Adrian Buckley and David Jenkins

CIRCA

'That's one small

step for a man,

one giant leap

for mankind.'

Commander Neil Armstrong, July 21st 1969

Ambition

The Apollo 11 mission begins as a challenge.
On May 25th 1961, President John F Kennedy
addresses a joint session of the United States
Congress in Washington DC. He says:
'I believe that this nation should commit itself
to achieving the goal, before this decade
is out, of landing a man on the Moon and
returning him safely to the Earth. No single
space project in this period will be more
impressive to mankind, or more important
for the long-range exploration of space;
and none will be so difficult or expensive
to accomplish.' But America is not the only
country aiming for the Moon. There will be
a race to see who can get there first.

Space race

In the eight years since President Kennedy's historic speech, the United States and the Soviet Union have launched manned space missions and an American has orbited the Moon. There are satellites in space, which can relay television pictures and international telephone calls. And on Earth, a new generation of aircraft can fly further and faster than ever before – 1969 alone has seen two 'firsts'. The Boeing 747, the world's first wide-bodied passenger jet, has made its test flight. So too has Concorde, the first supersonic airliner. Now NASA is about to seek another first – one that will fulfil President Kennedy's vision.

LIFE

16 PAGES OF FANTASTIC C
The Space Walk

Anticipation

It is Tuesday July 15th 1969. We are at Kennedy Space Center in Cape Canaveral, Florida. Far in the distance, on Launch Complex 39A, a giant Saturn V rocket stands out against the evening sky. Throughout the day, thousands of people have been arriving at the little town of Titusville, across the Indian River from the launch site. They will camp there for the night, eager to witness the event that will unfold in the morning. This is the eve of the Apollo 11 mission – the fifth manned mission of NASA's Apollo Program. It is the most daring yet. The entire world is waiting to see whether it will succeed.

Saturn V

The Umbilical Tower at Launch Complex 39A is as high as a thirty-six-storey building. It has two elevators and nine retractable arms, which provide access to each of the three rocket stages and the spacecraft for people, wiring and plumbing while the vehicle is on the launch pad. The arms will swing clear at launch. The Saturn V is the tallest, heaviest and most powerful rocket ever built. It carries fuel in three sections – rocket fuel and liquid oxygen in the first stage and liquid hydrogen in the second and third stages. It can propel a manned spacecraft deep into space.

Columbia

High on top of the Saturn V is the Apollo 11 spacecraft. Compared with the mighty rocket, the spacecraft is small and fragile. It is made up of three pieces. First is the Command Module, named *Columbia*, which will carry the three astronauts. Second is the Service Module, which will supply the Command Module with power, oxygen and water. Together these two elements form the Command/Service Module. The final piece is the Lunar Module, named *Eagle*, which for the launch is stowed safely in a conical Adaptor structure, which is located between the Service Module and the rocket.

Capsule

The Apollo 11 spacecraft is the most advanced yet built, but most of it will not survive the mission. The Command Module *Columbia* is the only piece designed to return to Earth. *Columbia* will be the crew's living quarters and the main nerve centre on the outward and return journeys. Inside this tiny capsule there is just enough room to stand up. Compact and ergonomically designed, it is packed with instruments – like the cockpit of an aircraft. The astronauts recline and sleep in adaptable couches, which will also protect them during impact on 'splashdown' at the end of the mission.

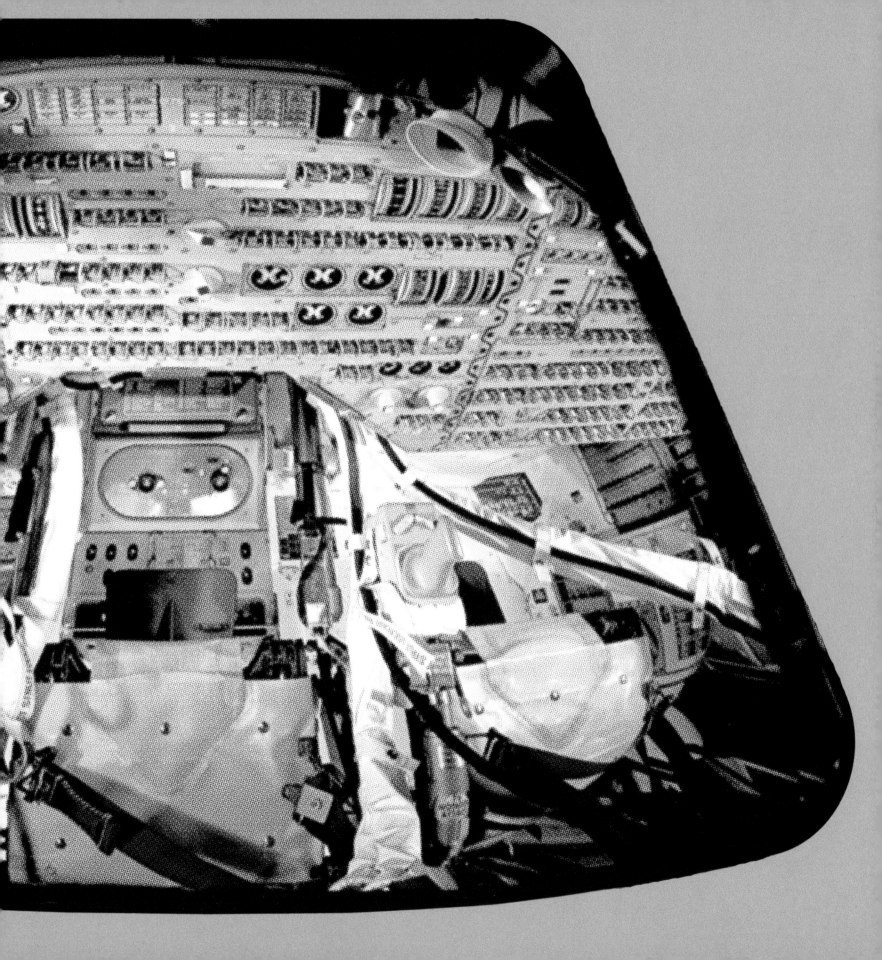

ARMSTRONG

COLLINS

Explorers

The Apollo 11 crew are Mission Commander Neil Armstrong, Lunar Module Pilot Edwin 'Buzz' Aldrin and Command Module Pilot Michael Collins. All three have journeyed into space before. Armstrong is an engineer and test pilot – a veteran of NASA's Gemini 8 mission. Aldrin is a fighter pilot. As pilot of Gemini 12, he was one of the first men to make an EVA – an extravehicular activity or 'space walk'. Collins is a fellow pilot and crewmember of the Gemini 10 mission, during which he made two space walks. These three men bring exceptional knowledge and experience to the mission.

Countdown

It is Wednesday July 16th – a perfect summer's morning. At 06:45 Commander Neil Armstrong takes his seat in the spacecraft. At 07:00, Michael Collins joins him. Buzz Aldrin boards at 07:07. Together they commence their pre-launch procedures. The Umbilical Tower's access arm retracts at 09:27. Everything is in order. Armstrong reports coolly, 'It feels good'. Shortly after 09:30, Launch Control in Cape Canaveral signals the final countdown ... 10 – 9 – 8 – 7 ... ignition sequence starts ... 6 – 5 – 4 – 3 – 2 – 1 – 0 ... all engines running, LIFT-OFF! The Saturn V rocket surges into the air.

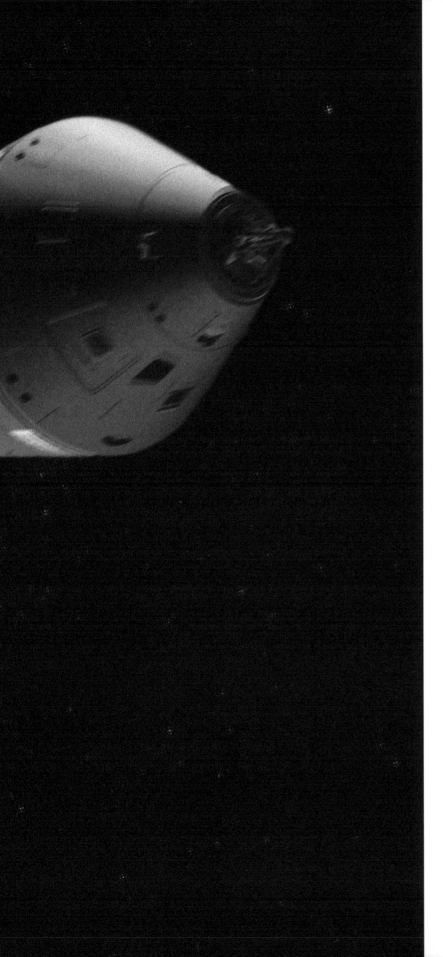

Trans-lunar injection

As the astronauts race away from Earth, fuel in the first two stages of the Saturn V rocket is burned and the sections fall away. Just 12 minutes after lift-off, the Apollo 11 spacecraft enters an elliptical orbit around the Earth. After one and a half orbits, the third stage of the rocket provides a 'trans-lunar injection' – a massive power boost that increases the flight speed to an incredible 24,000 miles per hour and sets the spacecraft on its final flight path. Neil Armstrong reports to Mission Control in Houston, Texas: 'That Saturn gave us a magnificent ride.'

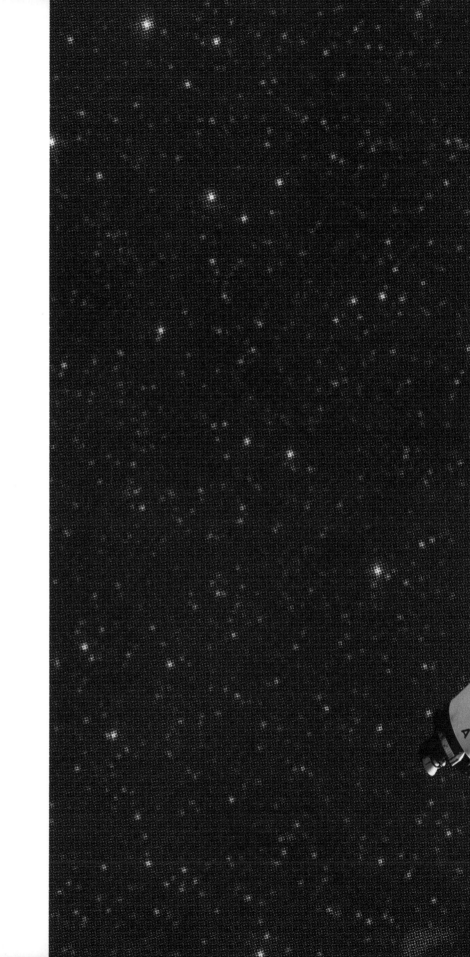

Preparation

At 3 hours, 11 minutes into the mission, the third stage of the Saturn V rocket has been released and the Command/ Service Module is flying under its own power. It is time to unite with the Lunar Module *Eagle*, which until now has been hidden within the Adaptor. The four panels that form the Adaptor shell peel open and fall away. Michael Collins turns the spacecraft through 180 degrees and gets ready for the docking manoeuvre, which he has practised many times on the simulator. *Eagle*, he says, is 'the weirdest looking contraption I have ever seen in the sky'.

PINEAPPLE
FRUITCAKE

Housekeeping

The outward leg of the journey will take three days. Life on board *Columbia* involves a series of housekeeping duties – charging batteries, dumping waste water, and checking fuel and oxygen reserves. Meals are prepared by adding water to dried food packs. Highlights on the menu are bacon squares and beef stew. Each morning, when Armstrong, Aldrin and Collins wake, Mission Control gives them a review of the day's news. They are keen to hear about the progress of the unmanned mission, Luna 15, which the Soviet Union launched on July 13th. Like Apollo 11, Luna's target is the Moon.

Approach

It is Saturday July 19th – day four of the mission. The spacecraft is on the final leg of its outward journey, accelerating now under the Moon's gravity. The Service Module's engine is fired to allow the spacecraft to enter an orbit around the Moon. Each orbit takes two hours. As they fly past, Neil Armstrong studies the landing site in the southern Sea of Tranquility. NASA has made maps of the Moon's surface, using data from the Apollo 8 and Apollo 10 orbiter missions and the Ranger 8 and Surveyor 5 landers. The Sea of Tranquility has been chosen because its surface is mostly level.

Eagle has wings!

It is Sunday July 20th – day five. Neil Armstrong and Buzz Aldrin are aboard the Lunar Module and the descent is going to plan. But wait – Armstrong notices that they are passing landmarks on the Moon's surface four seconds too early. They are heading for a crater! He overrides the computer and takes the controls, while Aldrin calls out altitude and velocity data. They correct course and touch down perfectly with just 30 seconds of fuel to spare. Armstrong's heart rate reaches 150 beats per minute – twice the normal level – but he reports calmly: 'Tranquility Base here … The *Eagle* has landed'.

One small step

It is Monday July 21st – day six of the mission – exactly 109 hours, 24 minutes and 23 seconds since lift-off from Cape Canaveral. Mission Commander Neil Armstrong opens the hatch in the Lunar Module and climbs down the ladder. He is the first person ever to set foot on the Moon – the greatest explorer in human history. A television camera mounted on the module captures the moment. The grainy black-and-white images are transmitted to some 450 million viewers around the world. Armstrong declares: 'That's one small step for a man, one giant leap for mankind.'

Spacesuit

The Moon has virtually no atmosphere. Without a spacesuit, Armstrong would not survive. The suit maintains atmospheric pressure, supplies him with oxygen and keeps him cool. The Apollo 11 spacesuit is a 'soft' suit, made from many layers of thin fabric. Metal rings at the wrists and the neck allow gloves and the 'fishbowl' helmet to be attached. The suit also has bags to contain human waste – NASA has not yet found a way of going to the bathroom in zero gravity. On Earth, the suit weighs 180 pounds. In space, of course, it weighs nothing. Armstrong finds his suit 'tough, reliable and almost cuddly'.

Moonwalk

Buzz Aldrin joins Neil Armstrong on the surface of the Moon. The lunar soil is slippery and their life-support backpacks are bulky, but both men are able to keep their balance. They take photographs, place scientific instruments, collect rock samples and plant a United States flag. After an extraordinary adventure, they climb back aboard the Lunar Module. Armstrong's moonwalk has lasted 2 hours, 31 minutes and 37 seconds; Aldrin's some 40 minutes less. They leave a plaque that reads: *Here Men from the Planet Earth First Set Foot Upon the Moon. July 1969 AD. We Came in Peace for all Mankind.*

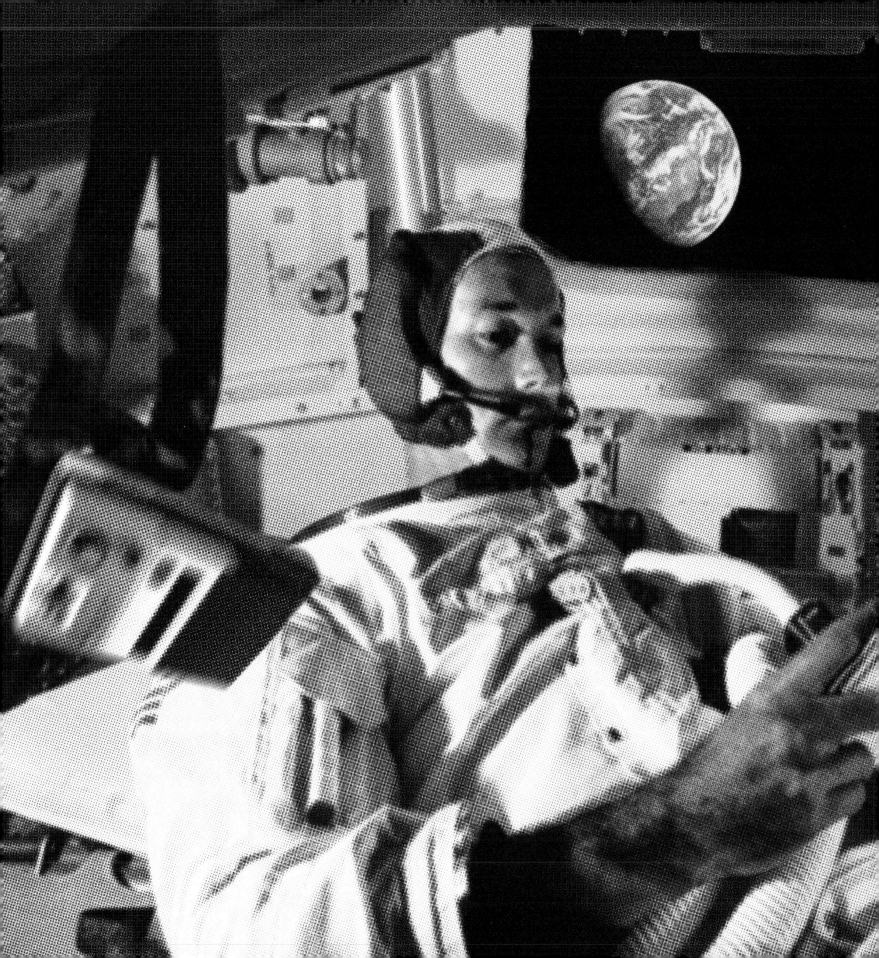

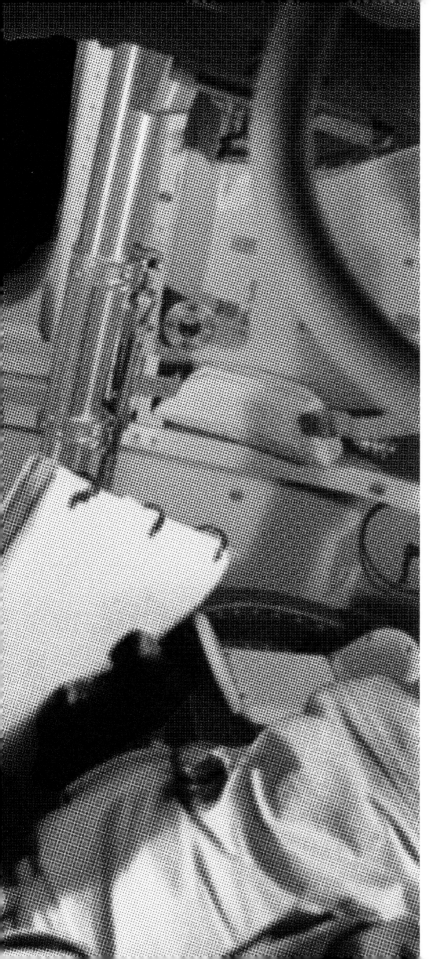

Solitude

For more than 28 hours, throughout Armstrong and Aldrin's epic journey, Michael Collins has remained alone aboard *Columbia* – the loneliest man in the Universe. For the 47 minutes of each lunar orbit when the spaceship is on the dark side of the Moon, there has been radio silence. He has waited anxiously to hear that *Eagle* has lifted off successfully. To his delight, *Eagle*'s arrival coincides with an Earthrise – the distant planet glows blue and welcoming in the sunlight. If everything goes smoothly, once the two astronauts have transferred, the Lunar Module will be jettisoned and *Columbia* will turn towards home.

Return

It is Thursday July 24th – day nine. Armstrong, Aldrin and Collins are safe within *Columbia*, plummeting to Earth at 20,000 miles per hour. Fourteen minutes before the spacecraft enters Earth's atmosphere, the Command and Service Modules separate. The astronauts are insulated from the heat generated on re-entry by *Columbia*'s thermal shield, which protects the capsule as it plunges through the atmosphere. In this final stage of the mission, there is little to do except watch and wait. Aldrin reports: 'Got our friend the Moon whipping by the field of view right now.' It is their last sighting of the Moon from the spacecraft.

Splashdown

At an altitude of 24,000 feet *Columbia*'s forward heat shield jettisons and drogue parachutes open. At 10,700 feet the drogues are released and pilot parachutes take over, slowing the capsule's approach to a gentle 22 miles per hour. It splashes down in the Pacific Ocean, just before dawn, a few miles from the recovery ship, *USS Hornet*. Neil Armstrong makes his final report as Mission Commander: 'Everyone inside, our checklist is complete, awaiting swimmers.' The Apollo 11 mission is over. It has lasted 8 days, 3 hours, 18 minutes and 35 seconds. Man has been to the Moon.

Cavalcade

It is Wednesday August 13th. New York City wakes up early to welcome the Apollo 11 crewmen. Armstrong, Aldrin and Collins are driven in an open car through a blizzard of ticker tape. It is the greatest parade in the city's history. Everyone wants to cheer the returning heroes. At times, the crowd almost engulfs the cavalcade. Later that day, the astronauts fly to Chicago for another parade and then on to Los Angeles for a state dinner, where President Nixon presents them with the Presidential Medal of Freedom. It is the beginning of an incredible tour that will see these three remarkable men acclaimed in cities all around the world.

Did you know?

Apollo
Founded in 1960, Apollo was the third human spaceflight programme undertaken by the National Aeronautics and Space Administration (NASA).

Room
The Apollo 11 Command Module provided 73 cubic feet (2.0 cubic metres) per person compared with 68 cubic feet (1.9 cubic metres) per person in an average family automobile.

Pieces
The Command Module had 2,000,000 functional parts, compared with 3,000 parts in a typical motor car.

Coincidences
Remarkably, Neil Armstrong, Buzz Aldrin and Michael Collins were all born in 1930; all were 5 feet 11 inches (1.8 metres) tall and all weighed 165 pounds (75 kg).

Samples
Neil Armstrong and Buzz Aldrin together collected 47½ pounds (21.5 kg) of lunar samples for return to Earth.

Gravity
The Moon's gravity is one sixth of that on Earth. The astronauts feel light-footed when they walk.

Veterans
Neil Armstrong, Buzz Aldrin and Michael Collins had each made a spaceflight before the Apollo 11 mission, making them the second all-veteran crew in spaceflight history (the first was Apollo 10).

Phone call
On July 20th President Richard Nixon spoke by telephone to Neil Armstrong and Buzz Aldrin on the Moon. The President called it 'the most historic telephone call ever made'.

Smells
Neil Armstrong said that Moon dust smelt like 'wet ashes in a fireplace'.

Armalcolite

One of the samples collected at Tranquility Base was a titanium-rich mineral named Armalcolite after Arm-strong, Al-drin and Col-lins.

Museum

You can see the Apollo 11 Command Module in the *Space Race* exhibition at the Smithsonian National Air and Space Museum, Washington DC.

Moonwalk

Neil Armstrong's moonwalk lasted 2 hours, 31 minutes and 37 seconds.

Science

Among the scientific instruments left behind on the Moon were a retroreflector array, used for the Lunar Laser Ranging Experiment, and a Passive Seismic Experiment Package to measure moonquakes.

Distance

When the Command Module was hoisted on board the *USS Hornet* it had travelled a total of 952,700 nautical miles (1.7 million km).

Fuel

The Saturn V launch vehicle carried 960,000 gallons (3.6 million litres) of propellant – enough to drive a typical motor car for 2.5 million miles (4.0 million km).

Quarantine

After splashdown in the Pacific Ocean the three astronauts spent 21 days in quarantine as a precaution against germs or diseases they might have brought back from the Moon

Men on the Moon

Between 1969 and 1972, Apollo missions landed 12 astronauts on the Moon.

Last visit

The last Moon landing was made by Apollo 17 in December 1972.

For Iris, who may one day fly to the Moon

David Jenkins is an architect whose writing ranges across disciplines. This is his second book for children. His first, *An Igloo on the Moon: Exploring Architecture*, won the DAM Architectural Book Award, 2015.

Adrian Buckley is a graphic artist, whose previous book for children, *An Igloo on the Moon: Exploring Architecture*, won wide critical acclaim. For *Moonwalk* he has created a series of illustrations rich with period detail.